Investigating spiders and their webs /
595.4 REN

220193

D060941Z

René,
7

T2-BQI-115

SCIENCE DETECTIVES

Investigating
Spiders and Their Webs

Ellen René

PowerKiDS
press.

New York

To my daughter, Laura, who weaves joy and laughter into my life

Published in 2009 by The Rosen Publishing Group, Inc.
29 East 21st Street, New York, NY 10010

Copyright © 2009 by The Rosen Publishing Group, Inc.

All rights reserved. No part of this book may be reproduced in any form without permission in writing from the publisher, except by a reviewer.

First Edition

Editor: Joanne Randolph
Book Design: Julio Gil
Photo Researcher: Jessica Gerweck

Photo Credits: Cover, back cover (top center, top right, middle left, bottom left), pp. 5, 6, 9, 10, 13, 14, 17, 18, 21 Shutterstock.com; back cover (middle center) © Jim Merli; back cover, (middle right) © Fat Chance Productions.

Library of Congress Cataloging-in-Publication Data

René, Ellen.
  Investigating spiders and their webs / Ellen René. — 1st ed.
    p. cm. — (Science detectives)
  Includes index.
  ISBN 978-1-4042-4482-5 (library binding)
  1. Spiders—Juvenile literature. 2. Spider webs—Juvenile literature. I. Title.
  QL458.4.R46 2009
  595.4'4—dc22

                              2007052803

Manufactured in the United States of America

Contents

Amazing Spiders

You have likely seen lots of spiders and spiderwebs. Have you ever wondered how a spiderweb got there? Have you ever wanted to know how a spider can drop down from above on a thin thread? If you have, you think like a scientist. Scientists wonder about the world around them. Like detectives, they ask lots of questions.

Scientists look for clues, collect facts, and study what they learn. Often they end up with more questions than answers. How would science detectives investigate spiders and their webs? First they would learn all about spiders.

This is a spiny orb weaver spider, also called a jewelled spider.
This spider uses its wheel-like web to catch bugs.

You can see the eight eyes and the mouthparts on this wolf spider. The two small parts in front that look like legs are really feelers, or palps.

How Can You Tell It's a Spider?

There are many kinds of spiders. They live all around the world. Spiders are **arachnids**. This means that spiders have eight legs and two body parts. Spiders have a hard outer covering, too. Their eyes, mouthparts, and legs are on the front part, or the **cephalothorax**. Their heart and silk-spinning **organs** are in the back part, or the **abdomen**.

Most spiders have eight eyes. Even with all those eyes, many do not see well. Special "hairs" on their legs and bodies help them sense their surroundings. Most spiders live only one or two years. Some big tarantulas live to be 20, though.

What Is Spider Silk?

All spiders make **silk**, even if they do not build webs. For their size, silk threads are stronger than steel. They stretch, or give, more than elastic. Spiders have silk **glands** in their abdomens. Spiders make **liquid** silk inside these glands. Different silk glands make different kinds of silk. Hunting spiders have four silk glands. Trapping spiders have seven. They use several kinds of silks to build their webs.

Silk glands connect to **spinnerets**, which spin the silk into threads. Liquid silk comes out of openings in the ends of the spinnerets. Scientists are not sure how the liquid silk becomes a solid thread.

This spider uses different kinds of silk to make its web. You can see some threads are very thin, and others are much thicker.

This spider has used sticky threads to tie up its prey. You can see the threads coming from the spider's spinnerets.

Different Kinds of Threads

Spiders make silk for many jobs. They can make strong, thick threads. Spiders use this kind of thread to tie up **prey**. Strong, thick threads also make the frame for webs and hold hanging spiders.

Spiders can also make sticky threads. Sticky threads in webs help catch prey. Stretchy threads keep webs from breaking when **insects** crash into them.

Many spiders make nests out of fine, thin silk. Female spiders place their eggs in a silk sac. To make the walls firm, the spiders crisscross the threads.

To get silk, scientists put spiders to sleep. When they tickle the spiders' spinnerets with needles, spiders spin out yards (m) of silk. Scientists study the silk to learn how spiders make it strong and stretchy.

Can Spiders Fly?

Most ballooning spiders do not travel far, but some spiderlings fly high and can end up hundreds of miles (km) from where the spiderlings started.

Spiders fly through the air without wings. How do spiders do this? They hitch rides on the wind! This is called ballooning. Baby spiders, called spiderlings, climb up high, stand on "tiptoe," and face the wind. They stick their abdomen in the air and make a silk thread. Air catches the thread and lifts the young spiders into the air.

Ballooning puts spiderlings in danger. Birds eat them. They may land in places where spiderlings cannot live. Why do they do it then? If they hang around the crowded nest, they are likely to be eaten by a hungry brother or sister!

This is a nest of newly hatched spiderlings. Soon these small spiders will balloon away from the nest and start life on their own.

A garden spider hangs from a dragline. Even baby spiders know how to make draglines and webs.

Draglines

As most spiders move from place to place, they trail long silk threads behind them. These draglines mark a spider's path. Spiders may use them to retrace their steps.

These thick, strong silks are the threads people see most often. Spiders use them to drop down from high places.

At spots along the way, spiders stick their draglines to things to mark their path and to keep them safe if they fall. These spots look like tiny white dots, and they are very hard to see. Draglines also form the frames of orb webs.

What Kinds of Webs Are There?

What happens to old webs? Spiders recycle them. They do this by eating their old webs before they make new ones! This helps give them the fuel they need to make the new web.

Spiders eat animals. They dine mainly on insects and sometimes on other spiders. Some spiders hunt for bugs on the ground. Others catch their dinner using webs. Spiders use many different kinds of webs to trap insects. Some look like sheets, funnels, or tubes.

Many spiders build orb webs to catch dinner. First they make the frame and spokes. Then they weave a **spiral** across all the spokes to make a net. Last they add sticky "catching" threads. Spiders use touch, not sight, to weave their traps. This is a good thing, since most spiders build their webs at night.

This is a funnel web. The spider hides inside the hole and rushes out when it feels an insect land in the web.

This crab spider is eating a fly it has caught. Crab spiders get their name because they walk sideways, as crabs do.

Do All Spiders Build Webs?

You may wonder whether all spiders build webs. The answer is no. All spiders have silk glands, though. All spiders create silk to wrap their eggs, too. However, some spiders hunt for food, instead of trapping food in a sticky web.

There are many kinds of hunting spiders. Some walk around looking for food. Others lie in wait. Crab spiders sit on leaves and flowers without moving. They stretch out their legs and wait. When yummy butterflies or bees land nearby, these spiders sense the movements and attack.

Jumping spiders have strong legs and good eyesight. They hunt during the day. Like cats, they quietly follow their prey and jump on it to make the kill.

Gotcha!

You may wonder how long it takes a spider to make a bug into its lunch. For many spiders, it takes less than a second to catch and kill their prey. Talk about fast food!

Generally, when a spider moves in for the kill, it catches its prey with the tips of its front legs. Then it pulls the prey to its **fangs** and bites. The spider's fangs inject **venom**. The spider wraps the insect in silk threads and starts feeding.

Spiders cannot chew. Instead, their fangs put something into their prey that makes its insides liquid. Spiders suck the liquid through a small mouth opening. When they are done, their victims are like empty boxed drinks with all the juice sucked out.

This crab spider is hard to see as it sits on a yellow flower waiting for its prey. It holds this bee with its front legs and injects it with venom.

Case Solved?

Have you found out everything you wanted to about spiders? Chances are you have thought of even more questions. For example, did you know that there are about 30,000 different kinds of spiders? Did you know that scientists have found spiders ballooning out in the middle of the ocean?

There is so much to learn about spiders. Have fun trying to answer your questions. Look for answers at the library or on the Web. Try to answer your questions by observing, or watching closely, the spiders that may share your house or backyard with you. You will find that spiders truly are amazing!

Glossary

abdomen (AB-duh-mun) The large, back part of a spider's body.

arachnids (uh-RAK-nidz) Types of animals, such as spiders or ticks.

cephalothorax (seh-fuh-luh-THOR-aks) A spider's front body part, containing its head and chest.

fangs (FANGZ) Sharp, hollow tubes that inject venom.

glands (GLANDZ) Parts of the body that produce something to help do a job for the body.

insects (IN-sekts) Small creatures that often have six legs and wings.

liquid (LIH-kwed) Matter that flows, such as water.

organs (OR-genz) Parts inside the body that do a job.

prey (PRAY) An animal that is hunted by another animal for food.

silk (SILK) Thread made by some insects and spiders.

spinnerets (spih-nuh-RETS) Parts, located on the rear of the spider's body, that make silk.

spiral (SPY-rul) A curved or curled shape.

venom (VEH-num) A poison passed by one animal into another through a bite or a sting.

Index

Web Sites

Due to the changing nature of Internet links, PowerKids Press has developed an online list of Web sites related to the subject of this book. This site is updated regularly. Please use this link to access the list:
www.powerkidslinks.com/scidet/spider/